The Presidency

by Patricia J. Murphy

Content Adviser: Professor Sherry L. Field, Department of Social Science Education,
College of Education, The University of Georgia

Reading Adviser: Dr. Linda D. Labbo, Department of Reading Education,
College of Education, The University of Georgia

Compass Point Books

Minneapolis, Minnesota

Compass Point Books
3722 West 50th Street, #115
Minneapolis, MN 55410

Visit Compass Point Books on the Internet at *www.compasspointbooks.com* or e-mail your request to *custserv@compasspointbooks.com*

Editors: E. Russell Primm, Emily J. Dolbear, and Deborah Cannarella
Photo Researcher: Svetlana Zhurkina
Photo Selector: Linda S. Koutris
Designer: Melissa Voda

Library of Congress Cataloging-in-Publication Data
Murphy, Patricia J., 1963–
    The presidency / by Patricia J. Murphy.
       p. cm. — (Let's see library. Our nation)
    Includes bibliographical references and index.
    ISBN 0-7565-0142-3 (lib. bdg.)
    1. Presidents—United States—Juvenile literature. [1. Presidents.] I. Title. II. Series.
    JK517 .M87 2001
    352.23'0973--dc21   2001001583

Table of Contents

Who Is the President?

The president of the United States is the leader of the country. He runs a part of the government. He protects the people. He helps keep the United States free.

The United States has had forty-three presidents. All the presidents have been men, but women can be presidents too.

What Does the President Do?

The president has many jobs. He helps to create new laws for the country. He also makes sure that people obey the laws. Sometimes he helps other countries work together.

The president is also the nation's **commander in chief.** He is in charge of the Army, Navy, Air Force, and Marines. He is the most powerful leader in the world.

◄ *President Jimmy Carter (center) helped the Egyptians and Israelis write a peace treaty in 1979.*

Who Helps the President?

The president's job is too big for one person to do alone. The president has many people to help him. One group of helpers is called the **cabinet**.

The members of the cabinet help the president solve problems. These people also help the president answer questions. They talk to the president about many subjects. They talk about education, transportation, and the environment. Fourteen people are in the president's cabinet today.

◄ *Members of his cabinet helped President Lyndon B. Johnson.*

Who Is the Vice President?

The vice president has an important job. He helps the president. He also works on special projects. He talks about ideas with the president and the cabinet. He travels to many countries to meet important people.

The vice president is the president of the **Senate**. The Senate is a group of people who write the country's laws. In the Senate, the vice president can vote to break a tie.

If the president dies or can no longer do his job, the vice president takes over as the president. Nine vice presidents have had to take over a president's job.

◀ *Vice President Al Gore (left) was also president of the Senate.*

Who Is the First Lady?

The first lady is the president's wife. The first lady helps the president in his job. Sometimes, she gives parties for important guests.

Eleanor Roosevelt went on trips across the country for President Franklin D. Roosevelt when he was sick. Hillary Clinton traveled around the world to help women and children. Lady Bird Johnson worked to plant trees and flowers across the country. Barbara Bush helped children learn to read. Nancy Reagan told people about the dangers of drug use.

◄ *Eleanor Roosevelt gave many speeches.*

Where Does the President Live and Work?

The president lives and works in the White House. The White House has 132 rooms. The president works in a room called the Oval Office. He meets with the cabinet in the Cabinet Room.

The White House has six floors. The president and his family live on two of these floors. Sometimes the family watches movies in the White House theater. They can play Ping-Pong or pool in the game room. They can also bowl or play tennis in the White House. They can swim in the swimming pool too!

◄ *The president of the United States lives in the White House.*

How Does a Person Become President?

The president is chosen by the people of the United States. The people select the president by voting. All U.S. citizens **vote** on the same day. This process is called an election. Election Day is always on the first Tuesday after the first Monday in November. An election for president is held every four years.

To become president, a person must have been born in the United States. The person must also be at least thirty-five years old. The person must have lived in the United States for at least fourteen years.

◀ *President Bill Clinton was elected president two times.*

What Does the President Promise to Do?

After the president is elected, there is an **inauguration**. It is always held on January 20. The president starts his new job on that day.

During the inauguration, the president makes a special promise. He puts his hand on a Bible. He promises to "preserve, protect, and defend" the laws of the United States. He must work to keep this promise to the people.

The president keeps this job for four years. Then there is another election. Sometimes, he is reelected. A person can be elected president only two times.

◄ George W. Bush was sworn in as president as his wife Laura watched.

What Does the President Mean to People?

The president is the leader of the United States. The people of the country trust him. They trust that he will protect them. They depend on him to solve problems. They depend on him to make good decisions. They trust him to be strong and tell the truth.

The president travels around the world. Wherever he goes, he speaks for the people of the United States.

◀ *President George W. Bush (left) met with Mexican President Vicente Fox.*

Glossary

cabinet—a group of people who help the president

commander in chief—head of the armed forces

inauguration—the event that marks the first day of the new president's job

Senate—one of the two houses of Congress that makes the laws of the United States

vote—to choose

Did You Know?

- The White House has 3 elevators, 7 staircases, 12 chimneys, 32 bathrooms, 147 windows, 132 rooms, and 412 doors!
- Before he was president, Theodore Roosevelt was a cowboy!
- President Franklin D. Roosevelt was the only U.S. president to be elected four times.

Want to Know More?

At the Library

Adams, Simon. *The Presidents of the United States*. Princeton, N.J.: Two-Can Publishing, 2001.
Pastan, Amy. *First Ladies*. New York: Dorling Kindersley Publishing, 2001.
Sullivan, George. *Mr. President: A Book of U.S. Presidents*. New York: Scholastic, 2001.

On the Web

Presidents of the United States
http://www.ipl.org/ref/POTUS/
For photos and facts about each of the forty-three presidents of the United States

The White House for Kids
http://www.whitehouse.gov/kids/
For information about the presidents and the history of the White House

Through the Mail

The President of the United States of America
The White House
1600 Pennsylvania Avenue, N.W.
Washington, DC 20500
To write a letter to the president and to learn more about the president and his job

On the Road

The White House
1600 Pennsylvania Avenue, N.W.
Washington, DC 20500
202/456-1414
For information about visiting the president's house, the Easter Egg Roll, and more, call
202/456-7041. The White House is closed to tours on Sunday and Monday.

Index

About the Author
Patricia J. Murphy has written many books for children includ-
ing storybooks, nonfiction, early readers, and poetry. She
received a bachelor's degree in journalism from Northern Illinois
University and a master's degree from National Louis
University. Ms. Murphy has taught in the Lake Forest public
schools. She lives in Northbrook, Illinois.